Know Your Emotions

HAPPY IS ...

by Connie Colwell Miller

CAPSTONE PRESS
a capstone imprint

Happy is a feeling
that we have from time to time.
Your tummy might get tingly,
and your eyes begin to shine.

2

Happy is a daddy's hug
when you and he have been apart.
You wrap your arms around him,
and happy fills your heart.

Good food fills your belly
and lasts for quite a while.
Happy found your taste buds
and made your mouth go "smile!"

6

Sometimes happy's peaceful,
like a walk outside with friends.
You look around at nature's gifts
and wish the walk would never end.

Happy is a game you play—
your friend goes first, then you.
Taking turns, you quickly see,
is happy shared by two.

People aren't the only things
that make your heart leap up.
Happy is a big dog hug
or a sloppy kiss from pup.

You might not know that happy hides
in work that's hard to do.
You try your best. You get it done.
You're proud—and happy, too!

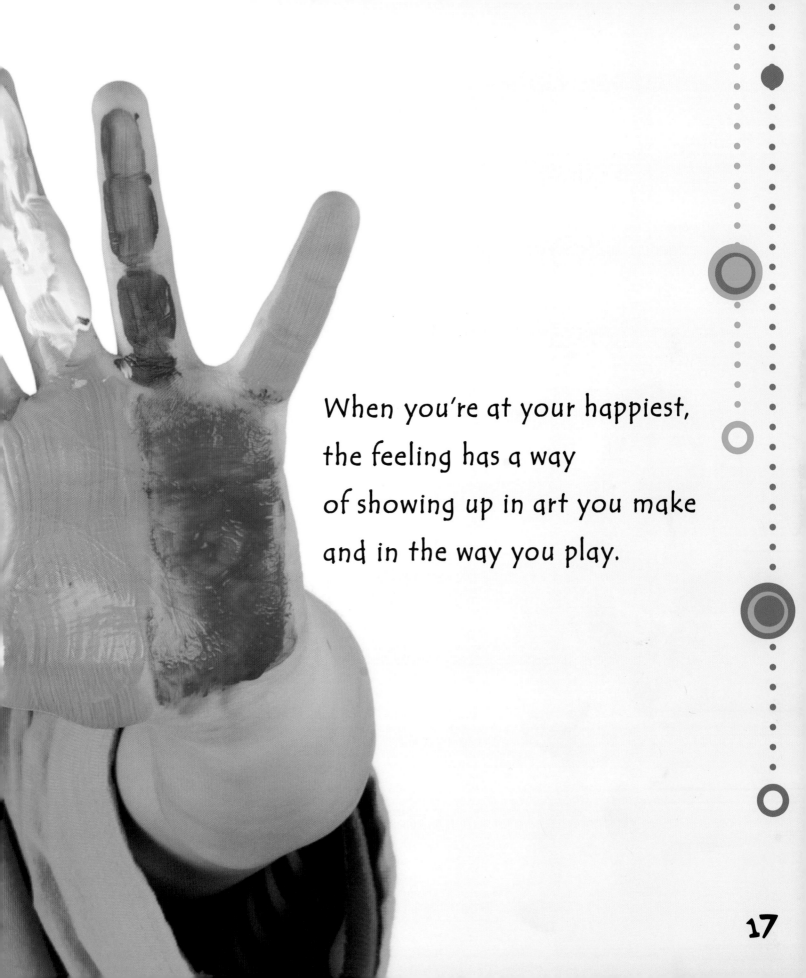

When you're at your happiest,
the feeling has a way
of showing up in art you make
and in the way you play.

Sometimes happy wiggles.
You feel the need to move.
When happy's tapping in your toes,
go ahead and groove!

19

Spending time with those you love
is the simplest way
for happiness to find you
each and every day.

20

Glossary

groove—to move with rhythm

peaceful—calm and happy

taste bud—a small bump on your tongue that helps you taste food

tingle—a prickly and ticklish feeling

Read More

Nemiroff, Marc A. *Shy Spaghetti and Excited Eggs: A Kid's Menu of Feelings*. Washington, D.C.: Magination Press, 2011.

McCloud, Carol. *Fill a Bucket: A Guide to Daily Happiness for Young Children*. Northville, Mich.: Ferne Press, 2009.

Meister, Cari. *Everyone Feels Happy Sometimes*. Everyone Has Feelings. Minneapolis: Picture Window Books, 2010.

INTERNET SITES

FactHound offers a safe, fun way to find Internet sites related to this book. All of the sites on FactHound have been researched by our staff.

Here's all you do:

Visit *www.facthound.com*

Type in this code: 9781429660426

 Check out projects, games and lots more at
www.capstonekids.com

INDEX

A+ Books are published by Capstone Press,
151 Good Counsel Drive, P.O. Box 669, Mankato, Minnesota 56002.
www.capstonepub.com

Books published by Capstone Press are manufactured with paper
containing at least 10 percent post-consumer waste.

Library of Congress Cataloging-in-Publication Data
Miller, Connie Colwell, 1976–
  Happy is... / by Connie Colwell Miller.
    p. cm.—(A+ books. Know your emotions)
  Includes bibliographical references and index.
  Summary: "Photographs and short rhyming verses describe how it feels to be happy"—Provided by publisher.
  ISBN 9781429660426 (library binding) ISBN 9781429670517 (paperback)
  1. Happiness in children—Juvenile literature. 2. Happiness—Juvenile literature. 3. Emotions in children—Juvenile
literature. I. Title. II. Series.
  BF723.H37M55 2012
  152.4'2–dc22   2011006126

Credits

Jeni Wittrock, editor; Alison Thiele, designer; Svetlana Zhurkin, media researcher; Sarah Schuette, photo stylist;
    Marcy Morin; studio scheduler; Eric Manske, production specialist

Photo Credits

Capstone Studio/Karon Dubke, 1, 4–5, 10–11, 12–13, 16–17, 18, 19, 20–21
Getty Images/Peter Cade, 8–9
iStockphoto/Chris Bernard, cover
Shutterstock/Dmitriy Shironosov, 2–3; Glenda M. Powers, 14–15; Zurijeta, 6–7

Note to Parents, Teachers, and Librarians

This Know Your Emotions book uses full color photographs and a nonfiction format to introduce the concept of being
happy. *Happy Is ...* is designed to be read aloud to a pre-reader or to be read independently by an early reader.
Photographs help listeners and early readers understand the text and concepts discussed. The book encourages further
learning by including the following sections: Glossary, Read More, Internet Sites, Index. Early readers may need assistance
using these features.

Printed in the United States of America in North Mankato, Minnesota.
032011   006110CGF11